The
Possibility
of you

ACTIVITIES FOR REINVENTION,
INSPIRATION, AND GROWTH

Dreams are renewable.
No matter what our age
or condition, there are
still untapped possibilities
within us and new beauty
waiting to be born.

DALE TURNER

Whatever age you are—16 or 60—you can always reshape how you define yourself.

To honor what has been and tap into what can be. This activity book offers a bridge between where you are and where you want to go. This is the messy, creative, and even beautiful place of rediscovery.

Maybe you're holding this book because of a big change in your life. You might be starting or leaving a relationship, or sending your child off to college. Perhaps you're moving to a new home after living in the same neighborhood for a long time. Or maybe there's simply a soft tug inside of you whispering, "What's next?"

Whatever the reason, you have a growing awareness that life holds many experiences and you will play many different roles within them. It's not about denying or dismissing parts of your experience. It's about celebrating all of you and creating something new.

There's no right or wrong way to use this book. No single answer for who you want to be. The prompts are designed to help you identify your own responses—this is a place for you to explore, experiment, and experience your own kind of rebirth.

Remember, these are natural and normal stages of growth. So breathe. Start from the beginning. You'll find your way forward.

Start —————

where

you are.

The first step toward creating something new
is acknowledging where you find yourself today.
And asking yourself why you picked up this book.
Maybe it's the overwhelming sense of too many
directions ahead. Or not feeling like you have
enough options. Or maybe you just need more
clarity to boldly take a step forward.

Now's the time to begin—when you look
around and turn toward something new

To Your Future Self...

What are some of the things you like about your life? What are some of the things that you wish were different?

_____

_____

_____

_____

_____

_____

_____

_____

_____

_____

_____

_____

_____

_____

_____

_____

_____

_____

_____

_____

NOW, IMAGINE YOURSELF A YEAR FROM NOW.

What's changed? What have you gained? What have you let go of? Write freely about why you started this activity book and what you hope will be true for you by the time you've finished.

Your life, right now,
today, is exploding with
energy and power and
detail and dimension...

Everyday Inspirations

What motivates you? You don't need clear answers to gain direction.
Just list as many things as you can: objects, people, feelings, values.

_____

_____

_____

_____

_____

_____

_____

_____

_____

_____

_____

_____

_____

_____

_____

_____

_____

Use this list to help clarify what you want. Notice which ones you
feel strongly about or call to you right now.

Take a snapshot of your life.

USING THIS "WHEEL OF LIFE," REFLECT ON DIFFERENT PARTS OF YOUR EXPERIENCE. Starting with the center as "not satisfied," and the outer edge as "completely satisfied," fill in each segment with how you feel about each area right now. Use brightly colored markers or draw simple lines with a pencil or pen—whatever approach best represents your thoughts and feelings about these aspects of your life.

HOW BALANCED IS YOUR WHEEL?

Is there one segment out of sync—part of your life that feels like it's missing something? Or are there several areas that you'd like to change or grow or become more satisfied with? Or is it something else not shown here (creativity, travel, or physical environment, for example)? Write down your answer(s) below.

_____

_____

_____

This is what needs your attention.

Take a step

you don't

your

even if

know —————————————

destination.

Someday is now.

Keep Moving

Studies show you are more likely to accomplish something if you simply write it down. Why not try it here? Look at your Wheel of Life and consider a goal or ambition you have and a small step you can take toward it each day in the coming week. The idea isn't that you will accomplish the goal entirely in one week. But this exercise is a great way to focus on what you want and move in that direction.

Sunday: _____

Monday: _____

Tuesday: _____

Wednesday: _____

Thursday: _____

Friday: _____

Saturday: _____

To accomplish
great things we
must not only act,
but also dream;
not only plan,
but also believe.

ANATOLE FRANCE

Get curious.

The secret to reinvention is welcoming your sense of curiosity, embracing a life of learning and growing, and staying flexible. Look outside of yourself for chances you can take. Look inside of yourself for creative inspiration.

By learning who you are and what you want, your priorities become that much clearer. It takes real courage to actively search within yourself. But dig deep. Experiment with your thoughts. Find a thread that you haven't seen before.

With just a little determination, each step will get easier.

All meaningful change
starts first in the
imagination and then
works its way out.
Therefore, dream often...
and dream big.

Envision Your Future

Create a vision of what you want your life to be: not just what it would feel like, but what it would look like. Are you alone or with someone? Are there new or different people around? Where are you living and working? How are you spending your days? What dreams have come true? Visualize and describe with great detail:

From
possible
to probable.

MAKE A LIST OF THINGS YOU WANT TO LEARN.

What are you curious about? What are some things you'd like to know?

_____

_____

_____

_____

_____

_____

_____

_____

_____

_____

_____

_____

_____

_____

_____

_____

_____

Does one of these topics excite you more than the others? Which one? Consider focusing on this in the days ahead and seeking resources online to help you get started. And remember: meet each learning experience with a beginner's mind—open and without expectation.

Tap into

inner

—— *your*

voice.

The things you are
passionate about
are not random,
they are your calling.

FABIENNE FREDRICKSON

Get to the Root

What is something you'd like to have or create in your life?
(Example: a more rewarding career.)

_____

_____

_____

_____

What would this mean for you?
(Example: better pay and job satisfaction or a happier and healthier family life.)

_____

_____

_____

_____

Do any of your answers shed light on your priorities or introduce
a new way of thinking?

_____

_____

_____

_____

One of the most courageous things you can do is identify yourself, know who you are, what you believe in and where you want to go.

SHEILA MURRAY BETHEL

Let go.

Sometimes, we carry old ideas with us into our new life chapters, but it's really our choice whether we do or not. For real change to happen, you must acknowledge who you are. You must take what you love and leave the rest behind—in the past, where it belongs. Now's the time to become resourceful, honest, and committed to who you want to become.

In the process
of letting go you
will lose many
things from the
past, but you will
find yourself.

DEEPAK CHOPRA

Accept and Release

What are some things you'd like to let go of?

Check all that apply:

○ Past negative experiences

○ Comparing myself to others

○ An old grudge toward someone

○ Resistance to trying something new

○ Fear of failure

○ Worrying about things that I can't control

○ Concern for what people think of me

○ A "need" that I've outgrown (Example: the need to always be right.)

○ _____

○ _____

Accept these elements as past ways of thinking or being. You can honor your history and appreciate its learnings—in whatever form they took—but no need to relive them here. You're doing the work to move on.

Make your own expectations.

"Should" is a small word with a big meaning. Over the course of one day, notice how often you say that you "should" do something, whether to yourself or out loud. We sometimes confuse old ideas or someone else's way of thinking as absolute requirements for our lives. Why not let go of the unnecessary "I should" with a renewed focus on "I could" or "I want"?

THINK OF THE EXPECTATIONS YOU HAVE FOR YOURSELF.

Are they yours or someone else's? What kinds of labels have you placed on yourself? Do you feel comfortable with all of them?

_____

_____

_____

_____

_____

_____

_____

_____

_____

_____

_____

_____

_____

_____

_____

_____

_____

You get
—— decide
right for

to ——————

what's

you.

The most beautiful people
we have known are those
who have known defeat,
known suffering, known
struggle, known loss...

ELISABETH KÜBLER-ROSS

Stronger Each Day

Are there past experiences that you wish you didn't have, such as a challenging relationship or something you regret doing? Are there lessons you'd like to share with your past self? How could you offer comfort and compassion to yourself now? Write to your younger self about these thoughts. Include anything you've learned that's helped you to grow and become stronger—that has brought you to the place you are today.

When I let go
of what I am, I
become what
I might be.

JOHN HEIDER

Build ——————
resilience.

What happens when you stumble? How do you practice patience and keep faith that you can weather change? Strengthen your resilience. Create consistency. Develop tools that you can rely on.

Remember this: failure is okay—and sometimes necessary. Forge the way as you go. Follow the roundabouts even if the direction isn't always immediately clear. Trust that it soon will be.

Making mistakes means you're stretching yourself into something new. Transformation can be uncomfortable, until all of a sudden, it isn't. The change itself becomes your new normal—what now feels right—and you can't imagine going back to an old way of thinking or being.

Every day of our lives
we are on the verge
of making those slight
changes that would
make all the difference.

MIGNON MCLAUGHLIN

One Thing at a Time

Stay motivated by focusing on little steps that lead to the bigger picture and strengthen your psychological resilience—your ability to bounce back when you stumble. Fill in each blank with a small way you can work toward your new life or an area in it you'd like to change.

○ CURRENT LIFE

Action: _____

Action: _____

Action: _____

Action: _____

Action: _____

○ VISION OF WHERE YOU WANT TO BE

Each of these is a breakthrough waiting to be celebrated.

Plan
ahead.

Create an insurance plan for yourself
when things go sideways. For example,
say you're working toward better health
and you've been running three times a
week. What do you do when there's
a thunderstorm? You could head to the
gym instead or perhaps use the time
for healthy meal planning.

IN WHAT OTHER AREAS OF YOUR LIFE CAN YOU "PRE-MAKE" DECISIONS SO YOU CAN FEEL SUCCESSFUL?

What I'm working toward:

A possible obstacle:

My contingency plan:

You always have the option to readjust, redefine, and try again.

Big change

——————————— small

It's okay

takes —————————

steady steps.

to crawl.

It's one of the simplest
sentences in the world,
just four words, but they're
the four hugest words in the
world when they're put
together. You can do it.

SHERMAN ALEXIE

A Better View

Our critical inner voice can be so loud, and seemingly
loudest when we are working toward something new.
Check the boxes of things you've told yourself in the past:

◯   "No one takes me seriously."

◯   "They're doing so much better than I am."

◯   "I'm not as qualified."

◯   "I'm really bad at this."

◯   "I can't keep up."

◯   "I look so stupid."

◯   _____

Now create your counterargument to the self-criticisms you've
checked. Some possibilities may be "I'm willing to try."; "They're
doing great, but I'm not doing so bad either!"; "I can do this."

_____

_____

_____

_____

_____

Come back to these new thoughts whenever you need a bit
of reassurance.

Let nothing dim the light that shines from within.

MAYA ANGELOU

Give ———————
thanks.

Practicing gratitude helps us gain a fresh perspective and enjoy a new attitude. Start by noticing the things that support and sustain you—this will keep you grounded in your new intentions.

Give special attention to the simple things that make you happy—your favorite pen, the steam from a shower, the view from your window. There is good in the everyday, no matter where you are on your journey. When you're in the middle of change, there's comfort in acknowledging the things that are already right in front of you.

Be content with what you have; rejoice in the way things are. When you realize there is nothing lacking, the whole world belongs to you.

LAO-TZU

All Around You

Using your five senses, take a minute to list everything around you—
the mundane, the obvious, the obscure. What do you notice? Is there
something right next to you that delights you? Your special mug,
the one that feels good in your hands; or an image on your cell
phone that makes you happy? How about a song that you heard
on the radio this morning that's stayed with you; or a subtle shift
in the weather that's lifted your mood?

Scarcity thinking.

We all fall into patterns that make us think we're stuck. *If only I had enough money. If only I had more time. If only...* Scarcity thinking, or the habitual fear of never having enough, is a common mindset. How will you reverse this tendency in your life?

FILL IN THE BLANKS BELOW TO START THE CONVERSATION
WITH YOURSELF:

When you think of becoming who you want to be, you sometimes
tell yourself, "I wish I could, but... _____

_____

_____ ."

What might be a way to reframe this thought and remove the sense
of lack? What can you do right now with the resources you do have?

_____

_____

_____

_____

_____

Moving forward, what are some other ways you can creatively remove
perceived obstacles? Writing down short affirmations, for example, is
an effective way to get out of thinking from a place of lack and keep
you focused on what you want.

_____

_____

_____

_____

_____

You ——————

—— are

enough.

What lies behind us
and what lies before
us are tiny matters
compared to what
lies within us.

RALPH WALDO EMERSON

Remember the Good

Think back on all the times you've cracked a puzzle in your life.
You have proven evidence that you are resourceful, adaptable,
and full of answers.

Think of a time when you faced a challenge. What was the obstacle?

_____

_____

_____

_____

_____

How did you overcome it?

_____

_____

_____

_____

What are some of your inherent traits that helped you?

_____

_____

_____

_____

_____

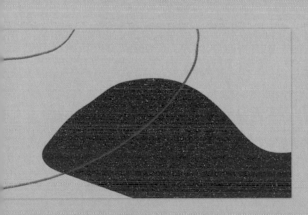

Shine with all you have.

KATELYN S. IRONS

Believe in yourself. —

What thoughts are holding you back? Maybe it's that you don't want to ask for what you want because you are sure you won't get it. Or you believe it's too late to pursue your innermost dreams. It can be easy for us to hold these kinds of beliefs as true statements. When in reality, they are often just that—beliefs.

Here's the thing about beliefs: you have the power to change them.

Why not imagine that you can absolutely ask for what you want? Why not consider that your whole life story isn't set in stone? You can create new visions that drive you forward. And you can literally reshape your reality based on what you believe.

When we believe
in ourselves, we
are free to grow
in our own soil, in
the direction of our
pure nature...

ALEXANDRA STODDARD

A Beautiful Garden

Gather all of your strengths below. Imagine this as a garden of all the good things you could harvest for new growth.

Adjust as needed.

Old beliefs sometimes creep back in
when we let our inner critic take over.
This can happen when we're tired or
feeling unsure about our next steps.

THINK OF AN OLD BELIEF THAT YOU TELL YOURSELF.
Maybe it's, "I'm not worthy of love" or "I'll be judged if I reveal my
true self." Write it down here.

_____

_____

_____

_____

Now write the opposite of that belief—for example, "I am worthy of
love" or "I'll be embraced for showing my true self."

_____

_____

_____

_____

Repeat this exercise when self-doubt moves in, and remember to be
gentle with yourself—reinvention is an ongoing process. Pause and
reset when you need to.

_____

_____

_____

_____

_____

_____

You are —
who you

think

you are.

Dreams not only
come true, they can
exceed your wildest
expectations.

TIFFANY LOREN ROWE

Dream Big

Think of a time when you had a plan, a goal, or an ambition that actually turned out much better than you'd hoped for. Now think of a new dream for yourself that you can start believing in. Write that dream down here.

_____

_____

_____

_____

_____

_____

_____

_____

_____

_____

_____

_____

_____

Hold the vision in your mind and consider writing it on a separate piece of paper and putting it in a place where you can read it often. It will anchor you in positivity and keep you moving forward.

Be your own
definition of
amazing, always.

NIKITA GILL

Finding your authenticity.

Acknowledging your current state of being isn't always easy. When a friend asks about a goal or dream you're working on, you say just that, "I'm working on it." But is this really true? How are you really "working on it"? Often our own feelings get in the way of taking the actions we wish to take. They act as barriers rather than as catalysts.

Your feelings require recognition in order to keep moving forward.

It's not about beating yourself up or falling down a shame spiral. It's being clear and bold, owning your journey, and turning your visions into reality. Here's where you can safely and completely be honest with yourself and follow through.

Your vision will become
clear only when you look
into your heart... who
looks outside, dreams.
Who looks inside, awakens.

CARL JUNG

Look Within

How would you describe yourself today? Think about the letter to your future self or the Wheel of Life you completed early on in the book and the areas that fell short of what you want in life. How do you feel about your answers right now? Are there ways in which you've grown or changed?

_____

_____

_____

_____

_____

_____

_____

_____

_____

_____

_____

_____

_____

_____

_____

_____

Notice what comes up for you and how it feels to write it down.

Recognize
how you feel.

When you acknowledge your emotions,
it helps you to fine-tune where you are
on your journey and what you may need
to keep moving forward in a healthy way.

IN THIS MOMENT, HOW ARE YOU FEELING?

Circle all that apply:

Happy	Confident	Sad
Content	Worried	Disappointed
Grateful	Delighted	Empowered
Ecstatic	Concerned	Cheerful
Lost	Optimistic	Satisfied
Scared	Joyful	Peaceful

_____   _____   _____

Spend a few moments reflecting on the words you circled or added.
What insights do you gain from your answers? The more you grow
in self-awareness, the easier it will be to understand what next steps
you can take in creating a life you love.

_____

_____

_____

_____

_____

_____

_____

_____

_____

_____

—— Be equal

and honest

parts kind
and true.

What is really hard,
and really amazing,
is giving up on
being perfect and
beginning the work
of becoming yourself.

ANNA QUINDLEN

Redefine Perfect

When we strive for "perfection," we're essentially saying there's always a right and wrong way to do things. Rather than worrying about a specific way to do something, perhaps you can find the perfect way for you.

What's something you worry you don't do "perfectly"?

_____

_____

_____

_____

_____

How does your way work really well for you?

_____

_____

_____

_____

_____

_____

Finding ways to be flexible with yourself leaves room to confidently accept who you are.

You are a child
of the universe,
no less than the
trees and the
stars; you have a
right to be here.

MAX EHRMANN

Be brave.

When we're younger, we hate being told what to do, but sometimes in life—particularly during times of transition—we yearn for someone else to show us the way.

We often look for guidance outside of ourselves, grasping onto something that might give us a cheat sheet. But only you know the right answers for you. Now's the time to tap into that place where you keep your courage, take the lead, and decide for yourself.

Find out who you are
and do it on purpose.

Focus

We live in a "busy" culture, where we value taking on multiple things all at once. Studies show that multitasking is not as effective as "monotasking"—doing one activity, intensively, at a time. Take charge and give yourself 90 minutes to focus on one task, with a 10-minute break in the middle.

What did you do? _____

_____

_____

Why did you choose to focus on this particular task?

_____

_____

_____

_____

How did it feel?

_____

_____

_____

Consider other ways you might be able to do things more purposefully. Part of reinvention is rediscovering your passions and focusing on them with care to create something new.

Embrace discomfort.

Experiencing change—no matter what kind—is almost always a little uncomfortable. We naturally resist it. And yet, it's the one thing in life that's inevitable. Though you may not be able to control change, you can control your own response to it.

TAKE A MOMENT TO REFLECT.

What's something that's changing in your life?

_____

_____

_____

_____

What are you worried about it?

_____

_____

_____

_____

What can you do about it?

_____

_____

_____

_____

How can you take ownership of the situation?

_____

_____

_____

_____

You can —— do hard

—— You have —— done them

things.

before.

We must discover the joy
of each other, the joy of
challenge, the joy of growth.

MITSUGI SAOTOME

Authentic Growth

Gain a new perspective and get feedback from someone you trust. You can simply ask, "How am I doing?" Request an honest response, sharing why you're asking for their thoughts. Here are some tips on receiving advice with an open heart and mind:

- Breathe deeply and center yourself
- Assume they have your best interest at heart and avoid getting defensive
- Ask clarifying questions and request suggestions

Whom did you ask?

_____

What did they say?

_____

_____

_____

Was it comfortable to hear?

_____

What did you learn about yourself?

_____

_____

_____

There is only one you. And you are important.

CHUCK SWINDOLL

Connect. ——

Reinvention is about connecting your past and your future. It's about the present becoming a bridge, linking the span of time.

Show your younger self what it looks like to live the dreams you had, to do the work you wanted to do, to feel the way you wanted to feel. You have the power to create the next chapter in your own life story.

...the foundations
of your childhood,
they stay with you.

CASSANDRA CLARE

Circle of Life

Brighten your day with the joys of your past. Close your eyes and imagine yourself as a child. Perhaps find an old childhood picture to reflect upon. Then take a breath... and get ready to play.

What's something you enjoyed doing as a child?

_____

_____

_____

How can you find time to do this again in the coming days?

_____

_____

_____

How did it feel to reconnect to that part of you?

_____

_____

_____

_____

_____

_____

_____

Look
back.

FIND A PICTURE OF A YOUNGER YOU.

Maybe even glue it to this page. Reflecting on that person in the photo, write a letter to them, sharing all of the understanding and compassion you have for that earlier version of you.

_____

_____

_____

_____

_____

_____

_____

_____

_____

_____

_____

_____

_____

_____

_____

_____

Rewrite

——————— expe

your ———————

ctations.

...it's never too late...
to be whoever
you want to be...

Hope and Dream and Imagine

7 things I hope for in the next 7 years:

_____

_____

_____

_____

_____

_____

_____

_____

_____

_____

_____

_____

_____

_____

_____

_____

Isn't it funny
how day by day
nothing changes,
but when you
look back, every-
thing is different...

C. S. LEWIS

Decide ⎯⎯⎯ on growth.

In the whirlwinds of life, we often rely on our immediate responses. Fight or flight, by the seat of our pants, impulsive behavior—these become our go-to stances rather than our last resort. Learn to be mindful of how you motivate yourself, and how to recognize and make thoughtful choices.

Notice when you're on autopilot. Instead, ask the right questions and take control. What are some things you absolutely have to do? What are some things you want to do? Are you happy with the choices you are making? Are there other things you could be doing instead? How will you live effectively, intentionally, day to day?

Life is what
we make it...

New Paths

As you continue on this journey of reinvention, think of all the
ways your awareness is growing. Perhaps you have a greater sense
of self—you know yourself a bit better and what motivates you. Or
maybe you have a better idea of what you want in the days, weeks,
and months ahead.

Use this space to capture a few things that feel different than they
did when you started this book—areas of your life where you've
created a different path or started something exciting or new:

_____

_____

_____

_____

_____

_____

_____

_____

_____

_____

_____

_____

_____

——————————— Positive
expectations.

TODAY HOLDS SOMETHING FOR YOU THAT YOU WERE ONCE LOOKING FORWARD TO.

What's one of these things?

_____

YOU CAN ALWAYS EXPECT GOOD THINGS TO COME. DELIGHT IN THE ANTICIPATION.

What are some things you're looking forward to now?

_____

_____

_____

_____

_____

_____

_____

_____

_____

_____

_____

_____

_____

_____

— Honor

you. ———

...find the positive in
every situation and focus
on that. What you focus on
becomes more pronounced.
When you zero in on the
positive, that's what you see
and that's where you live.

VICTORIA MORAN

Reflect with Love

Write or draw some things in the space below that you admire about yourself.

Come back to review and add to this page as your journey continues to unfold.

...there are so
many ways of
being alive in
this world...

KATIE ARNOLD

Praise the Journey

Go back to the letter you wrote to yourself at the beginning
of this book. Think about what you've given to yourself in the
pages in between. How you're making a difference in your own
life—with each new thought and every next step. Write yourself
a thank you note in the space below:

_____

_____

_____

_____

_____

_____

_____

_____

_____

_____

_____

_____

_____

_____

_____

_____

Every day you
reinvent yourself.
You're always
in motion.

JAMES ALTUCHER

Written by: Miriam Hathaway
Designed by: Justine Edge
Edited by: Cindy Wetterlund and Amelia Riedler

ISBN: 978-1-970147-58-2

1st printing. Printed in China with soy inks on FSC®-Mix certified paper.

Create meaningful moments with gifts that inspire.

CONNECT WITH US
live-inspired.com | sayhello@compendiuminc.com

@compendiumliveinspired
#compendiumliveinspired